FAVORITE BRAND NAME™

4-Ingredient
All-New
Recipes

All-New 4-Ingredient Recipes

Publications International, Ltd.

Favorite Brand Name Recipes at www.fbnr.com

Pictured on the front cover: Salsa Macaroni & Cheese *(page 72)*.
Pictured on the back cover *(left to right):* Roasted Chicken au Jus *(page 42)* and Arizona Cheese Crisp *(page 12)*.

ISBN-13: 978-1-4127-2437-1
ISBN-10: 1-4127-2437-6

Manufactured in China.

8 7 6 5 4 3 2 1

Microwave Cooking: Microwave ovens vary in wattage. Use the cooking times as guidelines and check for doneness before adding more time.

Preparation/Cooking Times: Preparation times are based on the approximate amount of time required to assemble the recipe before cooking, baking, chilling or serving. These times include preparation steps such as measuring, chopping and mixing. The fact that some preparations and cooking can be done simultaneously is taken into account. Preparation of optional ingredients and serving suggestions is not included.

Table of Contents

Introduction

Make meal planning easier with less ingredients! Cooking and baking can be difficult when there are too many ingredients to shop for, measure and prepare. Working with just four ingredients takes the stress out of cooking and meals are ready in less time.

The following pages are filled with the simplest easy-to-prepare recipes around. Most of these recipes include only four ingredients. That's right! Just four ingredients are needed to prepare delicious meals. There are, however, some recipes that have a few more than four ingredients. We aren't counting salt, pepper, water, nonstick cooking spray and small amounts of oil and butter, ingredients you already have on hand. Remember also that ingredients marked as "optional" or "for garnish" aren't included in the four-ingredient count— add them to make your meal extra special. These "extra" ingredients will add little time into your preparation since the amounts are so small.

This book is designed not only to make the recipes effortless, but to make finding the perfect one easy as well. The book is divided into five chapters, from appetizers for get-togethers to main dishes for the family. Another way to make cooking extra simple is by using the index. For example, if you have a certain ingredient on hand and want to use it for your meal, simply find the ingredient in the index and you will find many recipes to choose from. How much easier can cooking be?

Become the star of the kitchen when you serve these delicious dishes. No one will ever believe they were prepared with just FOUR ingredients!

Amazing Appetizers

Midnight Moon

Prep and Cook Time: 20 minutes

1 round (8 ounces) Brie cheese
3 tablespoons plus 1½ teaspoons crumbled blue cheese
2 tablespoons plus 1½ teaspoons coarsely chopped walnuts
3 tablespoons apricot preserves, divided
   Assorted crackers for serving (optional)

1. Preheat oven to 400°F. Cut Brie cheese horizontally into halves. Combine blue cheese and walnuts. Spread 4½ teaspoons apricot preserves on cut side of one half of Brie; sprinkle with half of blue cheese mixture. Place remaining half of Brie on top; spread with remaining 4½ teaspoons apricot preserves.

2. Wrap 3-inch high strip of foil tightly around Brie; secure with piece of tape. Sprinkle remaining blue cheese mixture over half of apricot preserves to form crescent moon shape.

3. Bake cheese in 8×8-inch baking pan 7 to 9 minutes or until soft and beginning to melt. Remove foil; serve immediately with crackers, if desired.

Makes 8 servings

Zucchini Pizza Bites

⅓ cup salsa
2 small zucchini, trimmed and cut diagonally into ¼-inch thick slices
¼ pound chorizo, cooked, drained and crumbled
6 tablespoons shredded reduced-fat mozzarella cheese

1. Preheat toaster oven to 400°F. Place salsa in fine mesh sieve and press out excess moisture; set aside to drain.

2. Place zucchini on toaster oven tray. Spoon 1 teaspoon drained salsa on each zucchini slice. Top with chorizo, dividing evenly among zucchini slices. Sprinkle 1½ teaspoons cheese over each slice.

3. Bake 10 minutes or until cheese melts. Turn toaster oven to broil. Broil 3 seconds or until cheese is lightly browned. Remove from oven and serve.

Makes 6 servings

Hurry-Up Turkey Roll-ups

Prep Time: 30 minutes

1 (3-ounce) package cream cheese with chives, softened
1 teaspoon prepared horseradish
1 teaspoon Dijon-style mustard
    JENNIE-O TURKEY STORE® Turkey Ham slices

In small bowl, stir together cream cheese, horseradish and mustard. Generously spread each turkey slice with cream cheese mixture; roll up. Cut into 1-inch pieces.

Makes 32 to 40 appetizers

Note: Recipe can be made up to 24 hours ahead. Cut into pieces just before serving.

Arizona Cheese Crisp

Vegetable oil for deep-frying
2 (10- or 12-inch) flour tortillas
**1 to 1½ cups (4 to 6 ounces) shredded Cheddar or Monterey
  Jack cheese**
½ cup picante sauce
¼ cup grated Parmesan cheese

Preheat oven to 350°F. Pour oil into wok to depth of 1 inch. Place over medium-high heat until oil registers 360°F on deep-frying thermometer. Slide 1 tortilla into oil. Using 2 slotted spoons, gently hold center of tortilla down so oil flows over edges. When tortilla is crisp and golden on bottom, carefully tilt wok, holding tortilla in place with spoon, to cover edge of tortilla with oil; cook until lightly browned. Rotate tortilla as needed so entire edge is lightly browned. Remove from oil and drain on paper towels, curled side down. Repeat with second tortilla. (Tortillas can be made up to 8 hours in advance.) Cover loosely and let stand at room temperature.

Place shells, curled side up, on baking sheet. Sprinkle each with half of Cheddar cheese; top each with half of picante sauce. Sprinkle with Parmesan cheese. Bake, uncovered, 8 to 10 minutes or until cheeses melt. To serve, break into bite-size pieces. *Makes 4 to 6 servings*

Chorizo Cheese Crisp: Remove casing from ¼ pound chorizo sausage. Crumble sausage into large skillet; stir over medium-high heat until browned. Drain fat. Follow directions for Arizona Cheese Crisp but substitute chorizo for Parmesan cheese.

Olive Cheese Crisp: Follow directions for Arizona Cheese Crisp but omit picante sauce and Parmesan cheese. Sprinkle ⅓ cup sliced pitted ripe olives and ⅓ cup diced green chilies over Cheddar cheese.

Sausage-Stuffed Mushrooms

4 ounces uncooked bulk turkey Italian sausage, casings removed
2 tablespoons bread crumbs
4 medium portobello mushroom caps
1 tablespoon olive oil
¼ cup shredded Asiago cheese

1. Preheat oven to 325°F. Crumble sausage into small skillet. Cook over medium-high heat until no longer pink; drain fat. Remove from heat and stir in bread crumbs.

2. Brush both sides of mushroom caps lightly with oil. Spoon sausage stuffing into caps, dividing evenly among mushrooms.

3. Place mushrooms, stuffing-side up, on baking sheet. Sprinkle 1 tablespoon cheese over each mushroom. Bake 15 minutes or until cheese melts and mushrooms are tender.

Makes 4 servings

Can't Get Enough Chicken Wings

18 chicken wings (about 3 pounds)
1 envelope LIPTON® RECIPE SECRETS® Savory Herb with Garlic
   Soup Mix
½ cup water
2 to 3 tablespoons hot pepper sauce* (optional)
2 tablespoons margarine or butter

*Use more or less hot pepper sauce as desired.

1. Cut tips off chicken wings (save tips for soup). Cut chicken wings in half at joint. Deep fry, bake or broil until golden brown and crunchy.

2. Meanwhile, in small saucepan, combine soup mix, water and hot pepper sauce. Cook over low heat, stirring occasionally, 2 minutes or until thickened. Remove from heat and stir in margarine.

3. In large bowl, toss cooked chicken wings with hot soup mixture until evenly coated. Serve, if desired, over greens with cut-up celery.

Makes 36 appetizers

Roasted Sweet Pepper Tapas

2 red bell peppers
2 tablespoons olive oil
1 teaspoon chopped fresh oregano *or* **½ teaspoon dried oregano**
1 clove garlic, minced
   Garlic bread (optional)
   Fresh oregano sprig for garnish (optional)

1. Cover broiler pan with foil. Adjust rack so that broiler pan is about 4 inches from heat source. Preheat broiler. Place peppers on foil. Broil 15 to 20 minutes until blackened on all sides, turning peppers every 5 minutes with tongs.

2. Place blackened peppers in paper bag to steam and loosen skin. Close bag; set aside to cool about 15 to 20 minutes.

3. To peel peppers, cut around core, twist and remove. Cut peppers in half; place pepper halves on cutting board. Peel off skin with paring knife; rinse under cold water to remove seeds.

4. Lay halves flat and slice lengthwise into ¼-inch strips.

5. Transfer pepper strips to glass jar. Add oil, oregano and garlic. Close lid; shake to blend. Marinate at least 1 hour. Serve on plates with garlic bread or refrigerate in jar up to 1 week. Garnish, if desired.

Makes 6 appetizer servings

Tip: Use this roasting technique for all types of sweet and hot peppers. Broiling time will vary depending on size of pepper. When handling hot peppers, such as Anaheim, jalapeño, poblano or serrano, wear plastic disposable gloves and use caution to prevent irritation to skin or eyes. Green bell peppers do not work as well since their skins are thinner.

Peppery Brie en Croûte

2 (4-ounce) packages crescent roll dough
1 (8-ounce) wheel Brie cheese
2 tablespoons TABASCO® brand Green Pepper Sauce
1 egg, beaten
Crackers

Preheat oven to 375°F. Work crescent roll dough into thin circle large enough to completely wrap cheese. Place cheese in center of dough circle. Prick top of cheese several times with fork. Slowly pour 1 tablespoon TABASCO® Green Pepper Sauce over top of cheese. Let stand briefly for sauce to sink in.

Add remaining 1 tablespoon TABASCO® Green Pepper Sauce, pricking cheese several more times with fork. (Some sauce will run over side of cheese.) Bring edges of dough over top of cheese, working it together to completely cover cheese. Brush edges with beaten egg and seal. Bake about 10 minutes, following directions on crescent roll package. (Do not overbake, as cheese will run.) Serve immediately with crackers. *Makes 8 to 10 servings*

Asiago Pepper Shrimp

24 large Florida shrimp, peeled and deveined
8 ounces asiago cheese
1 tablespoon chopped jalapeño pepper
12 slices bacon

Wash the shrimp and pat them dry. Butterfly shrimp by cutting lengthwise along the back-don't cut all the way through, leaving the tail section intact. Grate the cheese and mix with jalapeño pepper. Cut each piece of bacon in half. Fill the open section of each shrimp with about ⅛ teaspoon cheese mix. Wrap each shrimp with a piece of bacon, and secure with a wooden pick. Place shrimp on a broiler pan and broil until bacon is crisp. Turn the shrimp and broil until bacon is done. *Makes 24 appetizers*

Favorite recipe from **Florida Department of Agriculture and Consumer Services, Bureau of Seafood and Aquaculture**

Mariachi Chicken

Prep Time: 5 to 10 minutes   *Cook Time: 40 to 45 minutes*

1¼ cups crushed tortilla chips
1 package (1 ounce) LAWRY'S® Taco Spices & Seasonings
1 pound boneless chicken breasts or 2 dozen chicken drummettes
Salsa and sour cream (optional)

In large resealable plastic bag, combine chips and Taco Spices & Seasonings. Dampen chicken with water; shake off excess. Place a few pieces at a time in bag; seal and shake to coat with chips. Arrange in greased shallow baking pan. Bake, uncovered, in preheated 350°F oven for 40 to 45 minutes, until chicken is thoroughly cooked. Serve with salsa and sour cream, if desired.

Makes 4 main dish servings or 24 appetizers

Meal Idea: Serve with Mexican rice and/or refried beans and a crisp green salad or coleslaw.

Devilish Eggs

Prep Time: 40 minutes   *Chill Time: 30 minutes*

12 hard-cooked eggs, cut in half
6 tablespoons low-fat mayonnaise
2 tablespoons *French's®* Classic Yellow® Mustard
¼ teaspoon salt
⅛ teaspoon ground red pepper

1. Remove yolk from egg whites using teaspoon. Press yolks through sieve with back of spoon or mash with fork in medium bowl. Stir in mayonnaise, mustard, salt and pepper; mix well.

2. Spoon or pipe yolk mixture into egg whites. Arrange on serving platter. Garnish as desired. Cover; chill in refrigerator until ready to serve.

Makes 12 servings

Zesty Variations: Stir in one of the following: 2 tablespoons minced red onion plus 1 tablespoon horseradish, 2 tablespoons pickle relish plus 1 tablespoon minced fresh dill, 2 tablespoons each minced onion and celery plus 1 tablespoon minced fresh dill, ¼ cup (1 ounce) shredded Cheddar cheese plus ½ teaspoon *French's®* Worcestershire Sauce.

Buffalo Chicken Wing Sampler

Prep Time: 5 minutes   *Cook Time: 12 minutes*

2½ pounds chicken wing pieces
½ cup *Frank's® RedHot®* Original Cayenne Pepper Sauce
⅓ cup melted butter

1. Deep-fry* wings in hot oil (400°F) for 12 minutes until fully cooked and crispy; drain.

2. Combine **Frank's RedHot** Sauce and butter. Dip wings in sauce to coat.

3. Serve wings with celery and blue cheese dressing if desired.

Makes 8 appetizer servings

*For equally crispy wings, bake 1 hour at 425°F, or grill 30 minutes over medium heat.

RedHot® Sampler Variations: Add one of the following to **RedHot** butter mixture; heat through. Tex-Mex: 1 tablespoon chili powder; ¼ teaspoon garlic powder. Asian: 2 tablespoons honey, 2 tablespoons teriyaki sauce, 2 teaspoons ground ginger. Sprinkle wings with 1 tablespoon sesame seeds. Zesty Honey-Dijon: Substitute the following blend instead of the **RedHot** butter mixture: ¼ cup each **Frank's® RedHot®** Sauce, **French's®** Honey Dijon Mustard and honey.

Sweet and Sour Hot Dog Bites

½ cup SMUCKER'S® Concord Grape Jelly
¼ cup prepared mustard
1 tablespoon sweet pickle relish
½ pound frankfurters, cooked

1. Combine jelly, mustard and relish in small saucepan. Heat over very low heat, stirring constantly, until mixture is hot and well blended.

2. Slice frankfurters diagonally into bite-size pieces. Add to sauce and heat thoroughly.

Makes 20 snack servings

Splendid Soups & Salads

Quick Vegetable & Pesto Salad

Prep Time: 15 minutes

¼ cup mayonnaise
¼ cup refrigerated pesto sauce
1 tablespoon balsamic vinegar
6 cups assorted fresh vegetables from salad bar, such as sliced mushrooms, shredded carrots, red onion strips, sliced radishes, peas, broccoli florets and bell pepper strips (about 1½ pounds)
Lettuce leaves

1. Combine mayonnaise, pesto and vinegar in large bowl; stir until well blended.

2. Add vegetables; toss well to coat. Cover and refrigerate 10 minutes. Arrange lettuce leaves on salad plates. Top with vegetable mixture.

Makes 6 servings

Note: Chilling for 30 minutes will improve the flavor of this easy side dish salad.

Beef Caesar Salad

1 bag (10 ounces) ready-to-use chopped romaine lettuce
2 tablespoons fat-free Caesar salad dressing
1 boneless beef top sirloin steak (about 1 pound)
   Nonstick cooking spray
   Black pepper
2 slices whole wheat bread, toasted and cut into 32 croutons

1. Toss lettuce and dressing in large bowl. Divide salad greens evenly among 4 plates.

2. Cut steak lengthwise in half, then crosswise into ⅛-inch-thick strips. Spray 12-inch nonstick skillet with cooking spray and heat over high heat. Add beef; stir-fry 2 minutes or until beef is tender.

3. Top each plate of lettuce mixture with ¼ of steak strips. Season with pepper and top with 8 croutons.   *Makes 4 servings*

Serving Suggestion: Serve with tomato soup or a meatless vegetable soup such as minestrone.

Italian Vegetable Soup

Prep Time: *20 minutes*   **Cook Time:** *25 minutes*

1 package KNORR® Recipe Classics™ Tomato Basil Soup, Dip and
   Recipe Mix
4 cups water
2 cups sliced fennel or broccoli florets
1 large zucchini, diced (about 2 cups)
1 teaspoon dried oregano
   Grated Parmesan cheese (optional)

• In 4-quart Dutch oven, combine recipe mix, water, fennel, zucchini and oregano. Stirring occasionally, bring to a boil over medium-high heat.

• Reduce heat, cover and simmer 15 minutes, stirring occasionally or until vegetables are tender.

• If desired, sprinkle lightly with Parmesan cheese.

Makes 6 (1-cup) servings

Chicken Gumbo

Prep Time: 5 minutes   *Cook Time:* 20 minutes

3 tablespoons vegetable oil
1 pound boneless skinless chicken breasts, cut into 1-inch pieces
½ pound smoked sausage,* cut into ¾-inch slices
1 bag (16 ounces) BIRDS EYE® frozen Farm Fresh Mixtures
    Broccoli, Corn and Red Peppers
1 can (14½ ounces) stewed tomatoes
1½ cups water

*For a spicy gumbo, use andouille sausage. Any type of kielbasa or turkey kielbasa can also be used.

• Heat oil in large saucepan over high heat. Add chicken and sausage; cook until browned, about 8 minutes.

• Add vegetables, tomatoes and water; bring to boil. Reduce heat to medium; cover and cook 5 to 6 minutes.   *Makes 4 to 6 servings*

Italian Pasta & Vegetable Salad

8 ounces uncooked rotelle or spiral pasta
2½ cups assorted cut-up fresh vegetables (broccoli, carrots,
    tomatoes, bell peppers, cauliflower, onions and mushrooms)
½ cup cubed cheddar or mozzarella cheese
⅓ cup sliced pitted ripe olives (optional)
1 cup WISH-BONE® Italian Dressing*

*Also terrific with WISH-BONE® Robusto Italian, Fat Free Italian, Ranch, Fat Free Ranch, Creamy Caesar and Red Wine Vinaigrette Dressing.

Cook pasta according to package directions; drain and rinse with cold water until completely cool.

In large bowl, combine all ingredients except Italian dressing. Add dressing; toss well. Serve chilled or at room temperature.   *Makes 8 side-dish servings*

Note: If preparing a day ahead, refrigerate, then stir in ¼ cup additional Wish-Bone Dressing before serving.

1-2-3 Chili

2 pounds ground beef
4 cans (8 ounces each) tomato sauce
3 cans (15½ ounces each) chili beans in mild or spicy sauce,
    undrained
    Shredded Cheddar cheese (optional)
    Sliced green onions (optional)

Slow Cooker Directions

1. Brown beef in large nonstick skillet over medium-high heat, stirring to separate meat. Drain and discard fat. Combine beef, tomato sauce and beans with sauce in slow cooker; mix well.

2. Cover; cook on LOW 6 to 8 hours.

3. Serve with cheese and green onions, if desired. *Makes 8 servings*

Veggie Soup with Beef

1 pound beef stew meat
2 cans (15 ounces each) mixed vegetables
1 can (8 ounces) tomato sauce
2 cloves garlic, minced
    Water

Slow Cooker Directions

Place all ingredients in slow cooker. Add enough water to fill slow cooker to within ½ inch of top. Cover; cook on LOW 8 to 10 hours. *Makes 4 servings*

Mushroom-Beef Stew

1 pound beef stew meat
1 can (10¾ ounces) condensed cream of mushroom soup, undiluted
2 cans (4 ounces each) sliced mushrooms, drained
1 package (1 ounce) dry onion soup mix

Slow Cooker Directions
Combine all ingredients in slow cooker. Cover; cook on LOW 8 to 10 hours. Garnish as desired.

Makes 4 servings

Serving Suggestion: Serve this stew over hot cooked seasoned noodles or rice.

Shrimp Creole Stew

Prep Time: *5 minutes*   **Cook Time:** *20 minutes*

1½ cups raw small shrimp, shelled
1 bag (16 ounces) BIRDS EYE® frozen Broccoli, Cauliflower & Red Peppers
1 can (14½ ounces) diced tomatoes
1½ teaspoons salt
1 teaspoon hot pepper sauce
1 teaspoon vegetable oil

• In large saucepan, combine all ingredients.

• Cover; bring to a boil. Reduce heat to medium-low; simmer 20 minutes or until shrimp turn opaque.

Makes 4 servings

Serving Suggestion: Serve over Spanish or white rice and with additional hot pepper sauce for added zip.

Southwestern Soup

Prep Time: 1 to 2 minutes   *Cook Time:* 10 to 12 minutes

1 bag (16 ounces) BIRDS EYE® frozen Corn
2 cans (15 ounces each) chili
1 cup hot water
½ cup chopped green bell pepper

• Combine all ingredients in saucepan.

• Cook over medium heat 10 to 12 minutes.

Makes 4 to 6 servings

Northwest Split Pea Soup

1 cup USA yellow or green split peas, rinsed
4 slices bacon
1 quart water
2 cups leeks, trimmed and thinly sliced
1 teaspoon dried marjoram leaves, crumbled

Place peas in the bowl of a food processor for 1 minute to break up. Place into a 2 quart microwaveable bowl. Add the water, leeks and marjoram.

Cook the bacon in the microwave until crisp, reserving 2 tablespoons of the drippings. Crumble the bacon slices and set aside. Add the drippings to the peas. Cover and microwave on high 10 minutes. Uncover carefully and stir. Re-cover and let stand 15 minutes. Microwave the peas another 10 minutes at high power. Remove from oven, keep covered, and let stand 15 minutes before serving. Top each serving with bacon bits.

Makes 6 servings

Favorite recipe from **USA Dry Pea & Lentil Council**

Vegetable Potato Salad

Prep Time: 20 minutes   *Chill Time: 2 hours*

1 envelope LIPTON® RECIPE SECRETS® Vegetable Soup Mix
1 cup HELLMANN'S® or BEST FOODS® Mayonnaise
2 teaspoons white vinegar
2 pounds red or all-purpose potatoes, cooked and cut into chunks
¼ cup finely chopped red onion (optional)

1. In large bowl, combine soup mix, mayonnaise and vinegar.

2. Add potatoes and onion; toss well. Chill 2 hours.   *Makes 6 servings*

Clam Chowder

Prep Time: 10 to 12 minutes   *Cook Time: 1 minutes*

1 bag (16 ounces) BIRDS EYE® frozen Small Whole Onions
1 can (14 ounces) vegetable broth
2 cans (10 ounces each) clam chowder

• In large saucepan, place onions and broth; bring to boil over high heat. Reduce heat to medium; cover and simmer 7 to 10 minutes or until onions are tender.

• Stir in clam chowder; cook until heated through.   *Makes 4 servings*

Dilled Carrot Salad

Prep Time: 5 minutes

¼ teaspoon dill weed
1 can (8¼ ounces) DEL MONTE® Sliced Carrots, drained
5 cups torn romaine lettuce
   Honey Dijon dressing

1. Sprinkle dill over carrots in large bowl.

2. Add lettuce; toss with dressing.   *Makes 4 servings*

Sweet & Tangy Marinated Vegetables

8 cups mixed fresh vegetables, such as broccoli, cauliflower, zucchini, carrots and red bell peppers, cut into 1- to 1½-inch pieces

⅓ cup distilled white vinegar

¼ cup sugar

¼ cup water

1 packet (1 ounce) HIDDEN VALLEY® The Original Ranch® Salad Dressing & Seasoning Mix

Place vegetables in a gallon size Glad® Zipper Storage Bag. Whisk together vinegar, sugar, water and salad dressing & seasoning mix until sugar dissolves; pour over vegetables. Seal bag and shake to coat. Refrigerate 4 hours or overnight, turning bag occasionally. *Makes 8 servings*

Note: Vegetables will keep up to 3 days in refrigerator.

Inside-Out Egg Salad

Prep Time: 20 minutes

6 hard-cooked eggs, peeled

⅓ cup mayonnaise

¼ cup chopped celery

1 tablespoon *French's®* Classic Yellow® Mustard

1. Cut eggs in half lengthwise. Remove egg yolks. Combine yolks, mayonnaise, celery and mustard in small bowl. Add salt and pepper to taste.

2. Spoon egg yolk mixture into egg whites. Sprinkle with paprika, if desired. Chill before serving. *Makes 12 servings*

Hearty Minestrone Soup

Prep Time: 10 minutes   *Cook Time: 5 minutes*

2 cans (10¾ ounces each) condensed Italian tomato soup
3 cups water
3 cups cooked vegetables, such as zucchini, peas, corn or beans
2 cups cooked ditalini pasta
1⅓ cups *French's®* French Fried Onions

Combine soup and water in large saucepan. Add vegetables and pasta. Bring to a boil. Reduce heat. Cook until heated through, stirring often.

Place French Fried Onions in microwavable dish. Microwave on HIGH 1 minute or until onions are golden.

Ladle soup into individual bowls. Sprinkle with French Fried Onions.

Makes 6 servings

Strawberry Salad

2 packages (4-serving size each) strawberry-flavored gelatin
1 cup boiling water
2 packages (10 ounces each) frozen strawberries, thawed
1 can (20 ounces) crushed pineapple, drained
2 cups sour cream

Combine gelatin and water in large bowl; stir until dissolved. Add strawberries and pineapple; mix well. Pour half of gelatin mixture into 13×9-inch pan. Refrigerate until set. Spread sour cream over gelatin in pan. Pour remaining gelatin mixture over sour cream. Refrigerate until ready to serve.

Makes 12 to 14 servings

Appetizing Entrées

Roasted Chicken au Jus

1 envelope LIPTON® RECIPE SECRETS® Onion Soup Mix*
2 tablespoons BERTOLLI® Olive Oil
1 (2½- to 3-pound) chicken, cut into serving pieces
½ cup hot water

*Also terrific with LIPTON® RECIPE SECRETS® Savory Herb with Garlic or Onion Mushroom Soup Mix.

1. Preheat oven to 425°F. In large bowl, combine soup mix and oil; add chicken and toss until evenly coated.

2. In bottom of broiler pan without rack, arrange chicken. Roast chicken, basting occasionally, 40 minutes or until chicken is thoroughly cooked.

3. Remove chicken to serving platter. Add hot water to pan and stir, scraping brown bits from bottom of pan. Serve sauce over chicken.

Makes 4 servings

Slow Cooker Method: Rub chicken pieces with soup mix combined with oil. Place chicken in slow cooker. Cover. Cook on HIGH 4 hours or LOW 6 to 8 hours. Serve as above.

Sweet & Zesty Fish with Fruit Salsa

Prep Time: 15 minutes   *Cook Time: 8 minutes*

¼ cup *French's®* Bold n' Spicy Brown Mustard
¼ cup honey
2 cups chopped assorted fresh fruit (pineapple, kiwi, strawberries and mango)
1 pound sea bass or cod fillets or other firm-fleshed white fish

1. Preheat broiler or grill. Combine mustard and honey. Stir *2 tablespoons* mustard mixture into fruit; set aside.

2. Brush remaining mustard mixture on both sides of fillets. Place in foil-lined broiler pan. Broil (or grill) fish 6 inches from heat for 8 minutes or until fish is opaque.

3. Serve fruit salsa with fish.

Makes 4 servings

Tip: To prepare this meal even faster, purchase cut-up fresh fruit from the salad bar.

Nutty Pan-Fried Trout

2 tablespoons vegetable oil
4 trout fillets (about 6 ounces each)
½ cup seasoned bread crumbs
½ cup pine nuts

1. Heat oil in large skillet over medium heat. Lightly coat fish with crumbs. Add to skillet.

2. Cook 8 minutes or until fish flakes easily when tested with fork, turning after 5 minutes. Remove fish from skillet. Place on serving platter; keep warm.

3. Add nuts to drippings in skillet. Cook and stir 3 minutes or until nuts are lightly toasted. Sprinkle over fish.

Makes 4 servings

Glazed Pork Loin

1 bag (1 pound) baby carrots
4 boneless pork loin chops
1 jar (8 ounces) apricot preserves

Slow Cooker Directions

1. Place carrots on bottom of slow cooker. Place pork on carrots and brush with preserves.

2. Cover; cook on LOW 8 hours or on HIGH 4 hours.   *Makes 4 servings*

Serving Suggestion: Serve with seasoned or cheese-flavored instant mashed potatoes.

Slow Cooker Mesquite Beef

Prep. Time: 3 to 4 minutes   Slow Cooker Time: 9 to 10 hours

1 boneless beef chuck roast (about 4 to 5 pounds)
1 cup LAWRY'S® Mesquite Marinade with Lime Juice, divided
French rolls, flour tortillas or taco shells (optional)

Slow Cooker Directions

Trim fat from meat. Place meat in slow cooker. Pour ¾ cup Mesquite Marinade over meat. Cover and cook on LOW for 9 to 10 hours. Remove meat to platter and shred with fork. Return meat to slow cooker with juices; add remaining ¼ cup Mesquite Marinade. Serve shredded beef in warmed French rolls or in warmed flour tortillas or taco shells, if desired.

Makes 8 to 10 servings (or two meals of 4 to 5 servings each)

Meal Idea: Add your favorite frozen stew vegetables during the last hour of cooking for a pot roast/stew meal.

Lemon Rosemary Roast Chicken

Prep. Time: 10 minutes   *Cook Time: 60 to 70 minutes*

1 whole chicken (about 4 to 4½ pounds)
2½ teaspoons LAWRY'S® Seasoned Salt
2 teaspoons whole dried rosemary, crumbled
1 teaspoon LAWRY'S® Lemon Pepper

Rinse chicken with cold water; pat dry with paper towels. In small bowl, combine Seasoned Salt, rosemary and Lemon Pepper. Gently lift skin from meat on breast. Rub seasoning mixture onto meat under skin, all over outside of chicken and inside cavity. Place chicken, breast-side-up, in 13×9×2-inch baking dish. Roast in 400°F oven for 60 minutes or until meat thermometer inserted in thickest part of chicken thigh reaches 180°F. Let stand 10 minutes before carving.   *Makes 8 servings*

Hint: Loosely 'crunch up' some foil in the baking dish around the chicken to keep grease from splattering in the oven. Also, elevate the chicken on a cooling rack in the dish to help brown the bottom of chicken.

Chicken & Wild Rice Skillet Dinner

1 teaspoon butter or margarine
2 ounces boneless skinless chicken breast, cut into strips
    (about ½ chicken breast)
1 package (5 ounces) long-grain and wild rice mix with seasoning
½ cup water
3 dried apricots, cut up

1. Melt butter in small skillet over medium-high heat. Add chicken; cook and stir 3 to 5 minutes or until cooked through.

2. Meanwhile, measure ¼ cup of the rice and 1 tablespoon plus ½ teaspoon of the seasoning mix. Reserve remaining rice and seasoning mix for another use.

3. Add rice, seasoning mix, water and apricots to skillet; mix well. Bring to a boil. Cover and reduce heat to low; simmer 25 minutes or until liquid is absorbed and rice is tender.   *Makes 1 serving*

Wasabi Salmon

 2 tablespoons soy sauce
 1½ teaspoons wasabi paste or wasabi prepared from powder,
    divided, plus more to taste
 4 salmon fillets (6 ounces each), with skin
 ¼ cup mayonnaise

1. Prepare grill or preheat broiler. Combine soy sauce and ½ teaspoon wasabi paste; mix well. Spoon mixture over salmon. Place salmon, skin sides down, on grid over medium coals or on rack of broiler pan. Grill or broil 4 to 5 inches from heat source 8 minutes or until salmon is opaque in center.

2. Meanwhile, combine mayonnaise and remaining 1 teaspoon wasabi paste; mix well. Taste and add more wasabi, if desired. Transfer salmon to serving plates; top with mayonnaise mixture.   *Makes 4 servings*

Note: Wasabi comes from the root of an Asian plant. It is sometimes referred to as Japanese horseradish. It has a fiery flavor.

Dijon Baby Back Ribs

Prep Time: 5 minutes   *Marinate Time: 12 hours*   *Cook Time: 2 hours 10 minutes*

 4 pounds baby back pork ribs
 1 bottle (12 ounces) LAWRY'S® Dijon & Honey Marinade With
    Lemon Juice, divided

If needed, cut ribs in lengths to fit in large resealable bag. Place ribs in bag and add ¾ cup Dijon & Honey Marinade; seal bag and shake to coat. Marinate in refrigerator overnight. Remove ribs from bag, discarding used marinade. Place ribs on broiler pan that has been sprayed with nonstick cooking spray. Bake in 300°F oven until tender and no longer pink, about 2 hours. Finish on grill, brushing often with remaining Marinade, until glazed.
          Makes 4 servings

Meal Idea: Serve with corn on the cob, coleslaw and baked beans for a real barbecue treat.

Easy Family Burritos

1 boneless beef chuck shoulder roast (2 to 3 pounds)
1 jar (24 ounces) *or* 2 jars (16 ounces each) salsa
   Flour tortillas

Slow Cooker Directions

1. Place roast in slow cooker; top with salsa. Cover; cook on LOW 8 to 10 hours.

2. Remove beef from slow cooker. Shred meat with 2 forks. Return to slow cooker. Cover; cook 1 to 2 hours or until heated through.

3. Serve shredded meat wrapped in warm tortillas.   *Makes 8 servings*

Serving Suggestion: Garnish the burritos with any combination of ingredients, such as shredded cheese, sour cream, salsa, lettuce, tomato, onion and guacamole.

Bow Ties with Vegetables Alfredo

Prep Time: 5 minutes   *Cook Time: 20 minutes*

1 package (8 ounces) bow tie pasta, uncooked
1 bag (16 ounces) BIRDS EYE® frozen Farm Fresh Mixtures
   Broccoli, Cauliflower & Carrots
1 package (1.6 ounces) alfredo pasta sauce mix
½ teaspoon pepper

• In large saucepan, cook pasta according to package directions. Add vegetables during last 5 minutes of pasta cooking. Drain; return to saucepan.

• Meanwhile, in medium saucepan, prepare sauce according to package directions.

• Stir sauce into vegetables and pasta; cook over medium heat until heated through.

• Season with pepper.   *Makes 4 servings*

Variation: Stir 2 tablespoons prepared pesto sauce into alfredo sauce.

Serving Suggestion: Sprinkle with grated Parmesan cheese.

Ranch Crispy Chicken

¼ cup unseasoned dry bread crumbs or cornflake crumbs
1 packet (1 ounce) HIDDEN VALLEY® The Original Ranch® Salad
    Dressing & Seasoning Mix
6 bone-in chicken pieces

Combine bread crumbs and salad dressing & seasoning mix in a gallon-size Glad® Zipper Storage Bag. Add chicken pieces; seal bag. Shake to coat chicken. Bake chicken on ungreased baking pan at 375°F for 50 minutes or until no longer pink in center and juices run clear.   *Makes 4 to 6 servings*

Beefy Mac & Double Cheddar

½ pound ground beef
3½ cups water
2 cups uncooked elbow macaroni
1 jar (1 pound) RAGÚ® Cheesy! Double Cheddar Sauce

In 12-inch skillet, brown ground beef; drain. Remove from skillet and set aside.

In same skillet, bring water to a boil over high heat. Stir in uncooked macaroni and cook 6 minutes or until tender; do not drain. Return ground beef to skillet. Stir in Ragú Cheesy! Double Cheddar Sauce; heat through. Season, if desired, with salt and ground black pepper.   *Makes 4 servings*

Savory Baked Fish

6 boneless fish fillets, such as scrod, flounder or other mild white
    fish (about 8 ounces each)
¾ cup HIDDEN VALLEY® The Original Ranch® Dressing
Julienned vegetables, cooked (optional)

Arrange fish fillets in a large oiled baking pan. Spread each fillet with 2 tablespoons dressing. Bake at 375°F for 10 to 20 minutes, depending on thickness of fish, or until fish flakes when tested with a fork. Finish under broiler to brown top. Serve on julienned vegetables, if desired.

Makes 6 servings

Penne with Roasted Chicken & Vegetables

1 whole roasted chicken (about 2 pounds)
1 package (16 ounces) penne pasta
1 pound roasted vegetables, cut into bite-size strips
⅓ cup shredded Parmesan cheese
Freshly ground black pepper

1. Remove chicken meat from bones and shred. Discard bones and skin.

2. Cook pasta according to package directions; drain and return to pot. Add chicken and vegetables; toss together until heated through. Sprinkle with cheese and season with pepper to taste.

Makes 6 servings

Tip: Cook twice as much pasta as you need one night to get a head start on the next pasta meal. Immediately drain the pasta you are not using and plunge it into a bowl of ice water to stop the cooking. Drain completely and toss with 1 or 2 tablespoons of olive oil. Cover and refrigerate up to 3 days. To reheat the pasta, microwave on HIGH for 2 to 4 minutes, stirring halfway through.

Autumn Delight

4 to 6 beef cubed steaks
Olive oil
2 to 3 cans (10¾ ounces each) condensed cream of mushroom soup, undiluted
1 to 1½ cups water
1 package (1 ounce) dry onion or mushroom soup mix

Slow Cooker Directions

1. Lightly brown cubed steaks in oil in large nonstick skillet over medium heat. Place steaks in slow cooker.

2. Add soup, water (½ cup water per can of soup) and soup mix to slow cooker; stir to combine. Cover; cook on LOW 4 to 6 hours.

Makes 4 to 6 servings

Hot & Sour Chicken

4 to 6 boneless skinless chicken breasts (about 1 to 1½ pounds)
1 cup chicken or vegetable broth
1 package (1 ounce) dry hot and sour soup mix

Slow Cooker Directions

Place chicken in slow cooker. Add broth and soup mix. Cover; cook on LOW 5 to 6 hours. Garnish as desired.

Makes 4 to 6 servings

Serving Suggestions: This dish can be served over steamed white rice and topped with crispy Chinese noodles. Or, for a colorful variation, serve it over a bed of snow peas and sugar snap peas tossed with diced red bell pepper.

Easy Southwest Chicken

Prep. Time: 5 minutes   *Cook Time: 15 minutes*

1 package (1 ounce) LAWRY'S® Taco Spices & Seasonings
1 tablespoon lime juice
1 tablespoon BERTOLLI® CLASSICO™ Olive Oil
4 boneless, skinless chicken breast halves

In small bowl, combine Taco Spices & Seasonings, lime juice and oil; mix thoroughly. Brush mixture on both sides of chicken. Grill or broil chicken 10 to 15 minutes or until thoroughly cooked, turning halfway through cooking time.

Makes 4 servings

Meal Idea: Serve with Mexican rice and black beans. Guacamole and chips would complement the meal as well.

Variations: This marinade is also delicious when used on beef or pork.

Simply Delicious Pork

1½ pounds boneless pork loin, cut into 6 pieces *or* 6 boneless pork loin chops
4 medium Yellow Delicious apples, sliced
3 tablespoons brown sugar
1 teaspoon cinnamon
½ teaspoon salt

Slow Cooker Directions

1. Place pork in slow cooker. Cover with apples.

2. Combine brown sugar, cinnamon and salt in small bowl; sprinkle over apples. Cover; cook on LOW 6 to 8 hours.

Makes 6 servings

Tilapia with Spinach and Feta

1 teaspoon olive oil
1 clove garlic, minced
4 cups baby spinach
2 skinless fillets (4 ounces each) tilapia or other mild, medium-textured white fish
¼ teaspoon black pepper
2 ounces low-fat feta cheese, cut into 2 (3-inch) pieces

1. Preheat oven to 350°F. Heat skillet over medium-low heat. Add olive oil and heat. Add garlic and cook, stirring occasionally, until aromatic and tender, about 2 minutes. Do not burn.

2. Add spinach to skillet and cook, stirring occasionally, until wilted.

3. Lay fillets on lightly oiled baking sheet. Season with black pepper. Top each fillet with piece of cheese. Top cheese with spinach mixture.

4. Wrap one end of fillet up and over cheese and spinach filling. Pin down to center of fillet with wooden toothpick. Wrap other end of fillet up and over filling; pin down to center of fillet with toothpick. Repeat with remaining fillet.

5. Bake until fish is firm to the touch and flakes easily with fork, about 20 minutes.

Makes 2 servings

Spectacular Sides

Stir-Fried Asparagus

½ pound asparagus
1 tablespoon olive or canola oil
1 cup sliced celery
½ cup bottled roasted red peppers, drained and diced
¼ cup sliced almonds, toasted*
¼ teaspoon black pepper

*To toast almonds, place in small dry skillet. Cook over medium heat, stirring constantly, until almonds are lightly browned.

1. Trim ends from asparagus; cut stalks diagonally into 1-inch pieces.

2. Heat oil in 12-inch nonstick skillet over medium-high heat. Add celery; stir-fry 2 minutes. Add asparagus and red peppers; stir-fry 3 to 4 minutes or until asparagus is crisp-tender.

3. Add almonds and black pepper; stir until blended.   *Makes 6 servings*

Roast Herbed Sweet Potatoes
with Bacon & Onions

3 thick slices applewood-smoked bacon or peppered bacon, diced
2 pounds sweet potatoes, peeled and cut into 2-inch chunks
2 medium onions, cut into 8 wedges
1 teaspoon salt
1 teaspoon dried thyme
¼ teaspoon black pepper

1. Preheat oven to 375°F. Cook bacon in large, deep skillet until crisp. Remove from heat. Transfer bacon to paper towels to drain; set aside. Add potatoes and onions to drippings in skillet; toss until coated. Stir in salt, thyme and pepper.

2. Spread mixture in single layer on ungreased 15×10-inch jelly-roll pan or shallow roasting pan. Bake 40 to 50 minutes or until golden brown and tender. Transfer to serving bowl; sprinkle with bacon.

Makes 10 to 12 servings

Knorr French Onion-Roasted Potatoes

Prep Time: *10 minutes*   **Cook Time:** *35 minutes*

¼ cup BERTOLLI® CLASSICO™ Olive Oil
1 package KNORR® Recipe Classics™ French Onion Soup, Dip and Recipe Mix
½ teaspoon dried rosemary, crumbled (optional)
4 medium all-purpose or red bliss potatoes, cut into large chunks (about 2 pounds)

Preheat oven to 425°F. In bottom of broiler pan or in 13×9-inch baking or roasting pan, combine all ingredients.

Bake uncovered, stirring occasionally, 35 minutes or until potatoes are tender and golden brown.

Makes 8 servings

Cauliflower with Onion Butter

1 cup (2 sticks) butter, divided
1 cup diced onion
1 head cauliflower, cut into 2½×2-inch florets
½ cup water

1. Melt ½ cup butter in a 10-inch skillet over medium heat. Add onion and cook, stirring occasionally, until onion browns (about 20 minutes).

2. Meanwhile, place cauliflower and water in microwavable container. Microwave on HIGH 8 minutes or until crisp-tender.

3. Add remaining butter to skillet with onions and cook, stirring frequently, until melted and well blended. Pour over cooked cauliflower and serve immediately.
Makes 18 (½-cup) servings

Broiled Ranch Mushrooms

1 pound medium mushrooms
**1 packet (1 ounce) HIDDEN VALLEY® The Original Ranch® Salad
   Dressing & Seasoning Mix**
¼ cup vegetable oil
¼ cup water
1 tablespoon balsamic vinegar

Place mushrooms in a gallon-size Glad® Zipper Storage Bag. Whisk together salad dressing & seasoning mix, oil, water and vinegar. Pour over mushrooms; seal bag and marinate in refrigerator for 30 minutes, turning occasionally. Place mushrooms on a broiling rack. Broil 4 inches from heat for about 8 minutes or until tender.
Makes 4 to 6 servings

Oven-Roasted Asparagus

   1 bunch (12 to 14 ounces) asparagus spears
   1 tablespoon olive oil
   ½ teaspoon salt
   ¼ teaspoon black pepper
   ¼ cup shredded Asiago or Parmesan cheese

1. Preheat oven to 425°F.

2. Trim off and discard tough ends of asparagus spears. Peel stem ends with vegetable peeler, if desired. Arrange asparagus in shallow baking dish. Drizzle oil over asparagus; turn stalks to coat. Sprinkle with salt and pepper.

3. Roast asparagus until tender, about 12 to 18 minutes depending on thickness of asparagus. Chop or leave spears whole. Sprinkle with cheese.

Makes 4 servings

Leeks with Bel Paese®

   3 leeks
   3 tablespoons butter
   1 tablespoon olive oil
   2 cups milk
   4 ounces BEL PAESE® semi-soft cheese, thinly sliced
   Pepper

To prepare leeks
Remove tops to within 2 inches of bulb. Remove outer layer of bulb. Wash leeks thoroughly. Cut into large pieces.

In medium saucepan, melt butter over medium-low heat. Add oil, milk and leeks. Cover and cook until tender, 20 to 30 minutes. Drain thoroughly.

Preheat oven to 350°F. Butter 1-quart casserole. Place leeks in prepared casserole. Cover with slices of cheese. Bake until cheese is melted, 10 to 15 minutes. Sprinkle with pepper to taste. Serve immediately.

Makes 4 servings

1-2-3 Cheddar Broccoli Casserole

Prep Time: 5 minutes   *Cook Time: 20 minutes*

1 jar (1 pound) RAGÚ® Cheesy!® Double Cheddar Sauce
2 boxes (10 ounces each) frozen broccoli florets, thawed
¼ cup plain or Italian seasoned dry bread crumbs
1 tablespoon I CAN'T BELIEVE IT'S NOT BUTTER!® Spread, melted

Preheat oven to 350°F. In 1½-quart casserole, combine Ragú Cheesy! Sauce and broccoli.

Evenly top with bread crumbs combined with Spread.

Bake uncovered 20 minutes or until bread crumbs are golden and broccoli is tender.   *Makes 6 servings*

Tip: Substitute your favorite frozen vegetables or vegetable blend for broccoli florets.

Oven-Roasted Vegetables

1½ pounds assorted cut-up fresh vegetables*
3 tablespoons I CAN'T BELIEVE IT'S NOT BUTTER!® Spread, melted
2 cloves garlic, finely chopped
1 tablespoon chopped fresh oregano leaves *or* 1 teaspoon dried
    oregano leaves, crushed
Salt and ground black pepper to taste

*Use any combination of the following: zucchini, red, green or yellow bell peppers, Spanish or red onions, white or portobello mushrooms and carrots.

Preheat oven to 450°F.

In bottom of broiler pan, without rack, combine all ingredients. Roast 20 minutes or until vegetables are tender, stirring once.   *Makes 4 servings*

Scalloped Garlic Potatoes

3 medium all-purpose potatoes, peeled and thinly sliced
   (about 1½ pounds)
1 envelope LIPTON® RECIPE SECRETS® Savory Herb with Garlic
   Soup Mix
1 cup (½ pint) whipping or heavy cream
½ cup water

1. Preheat oven to 375°F. In lightly greased 2-quart shallow baking dish, arrange potatoes. In medium bowl, blend remaining ingredients; pour over potatoes.

2. Bake, uncovered, 45 minutes or until potatoes are tender.

Makes 4 servings

Salsa Macaroni & Cheese

Prep Time: *5 minutes*   **Cook Time:** *15 minutes*

1 jar (1 pound) RAGÚ® Cheese Creations!® Double Cheddar Sauce
1 cup prepared mild salsa
8 ounces elbow macaroni, cooked and drained

1. In 2-quart saucepan, heat Ragú Cheese Creations! Sauce over medium heat. Stir in salsa; heat through.

2. Toss with hot macaroni. Serve immediately.

Makes 4 servings

Savory Skillet Broccoli

Prep Time: 5 minutes   *Cook Time: 10 minutes*

1 tablespoon BERTOLLI® Olive Oil
6 cups fresh broccoli florets *or* 1 pound green beans, trimmed
1 envelope LIPTON® RECIPE SECRETS® Golden Onion Soup Mix*
1½ cups water

*Also terrific with LIPTON® RECIPE SECRETS® Onion Mushroom Soup Mix.

1. In 12-inch skillet, heat oil over medium-high heat and cook broccoli, stirring occasionally, 2 minutes.

2. Stir in soup mix blended with water. Bring to a boil over high heat.

3. Reduce heat to medium-low and simmer covered 6 minutes or until broccoli is tender.   *Makes 4 servings*

Microwave Sweet Potato Chips

2 cups thinly sliced sweet potatoes
1 tablespoon packed brown sugar
2 teaspoons margarine

Microwave Directions
Place sweet potatoes in single layer in microwavable dish. Sprinkle with water. Microwave at HIGH 5 minutes. Stir in brown sugar and margarine. Microwave at HIGH 2 to 3 minutes. Let stand a few minutes before serving.

Makes 4 servings

Favorite recipe from **The Sugar Association, Inc.**

Delectable Desserts

Ricotta Cheese and Blueberry Parfait

1 cup whole milk ricotta cheese
1 tablespoon powdered sugar
Grated peel of 1 lemon
1½ cups fresh blueberries

Combine ricotta cheese, sugar and lemon peel in medium bowl; mix well. Place 3 tablespoons blueberries in each of 4 parfait glasses. Add ¼ cup ricotta cheese mixture; top with another 3 tablespoons blueberries. Garnish as desired.

Makes 4 parfaits

Angel Food Cake with Blueberry Yogurt Sauce

½ cup frozen blueberries
Purchased small round angel food cake
½ cup vanilla nonfat yogurt
1 tablespoon granulated sugar
1 teaspoon lemon juice

Allow blueberries to thaw slightly. Cut angel food cake into 12 slices. Stir together yogurt, sugar and lemon juice in small bowl. To serve, spoon yogurt mixture and blueberries evenly over cake slices.

Makes 12 servings

Favorite recipe from **The Sugar Association, Inc.**

Fluted Kisses® Cups with Peanut Butter Filling

72 HERSHEY'S KISSES® Brand Milk Chocolates, divided
1 cup REESE'S® Creamy Peanut Butter
1 cup powdered sugar
1 tablespoon butter or margarine, softened

1. Line small baking cups (1¾ inches in diameter) with small paper baking liners. Remove wrappers from chocolates.

2. Place 48 chocolates in small microwave-safe bowl. Microwave on HIGH (100%) 1 minute or until chocolate is melted and smooth when stirred. Using small brush, coat inside of paper cups with melted chocolate.

3. Refrigerate 20 minutes; reapply melted chocolate to any thin spots. Refrigerate until firm, preferably overnight. Gently peel paper from chocolate cups.

4. Beat peanut butter, powdered sugar and butter with electric mixer on medium speed in small bowl until smooth. Spoon into chocolate cups. Before serving, top each cup with a chocolate piece. Cover; store cups in refrigerator.

Makes about 2 dozen pieces

Amy's Lemonade Mousse

1 quart cold milk
2 packages (1 ounce each) vanilla instant pudding mix
2 packages (½ ounce each) powdered lemonade mix, undiluted
1 container (8 ounces) frozen whipped topping, thawed
Fresh or frozen mixed berries

1. Pour milk into large mixing bowl. Add pudding mix and whisk for 2 minutes until smooth. Whisk in powdered lemonade mix. After mixture thickens, whisk in whipped topping until smooth. Pour into 8 parfait glasses. Chill.

2. Garnish with berries.

Makes 8 servings

Chocolate Truffle Cups

1 (7-ounce) package ALOUETTE® Crème Fraîche
8 ounces good quality white or bittersweet chocolate broken into
   small pieces
1 tablespoon liqueur, such as almond, coffee or orange (optional)
1 (2-ounce) package frozen mini phyllo shells

Heat crème fraîche over medium heat until it softens to a thick liquid consistency. Remove from heat and add chocolate. Stir until chocolate is melted and mixture is smooth. Add liqueur if desired. Refrigerate for 1 hour or until set. Pipe into phyllo shells and serve.   *Makes 15 dessert cups*

Dipsy Doodles Butterscotch Dip

Prep Time: *15 minutes*

1 (14-ounce) can EAGLE BRAND® Sweetened Condensed Milk
   (NOT evaporated milk)
1½ cups milk
1 (4-serving-size) package cook-and-serve butterscotch pudding
   and pie filling mix
Apples or pears, cored and sliced, or banana chunks

1. In medium saucepan over medium heat, combine EAGLE BRAND®, milk and pudding mix. Cook and stir until thickened and bubbly; cook 2 minutes more.

2. Cool slightly. Pour into serving bowl or individual cups. Serve warm with fruit.   *Makes about 2½ cups dip*

Tip: Store leftovers covered in the refrigerator. Reheat and serve as a sauce over vanilla ice cream. Sprinkle sauce with miniature semi-sweet chocolate chips or toasted nuts, if desired.

Easy Raspberry Ice Cream

1¾ cups frozen unsweetened raspberries
2 to 3 tablespoons powdered sugar
½ cup whipping cream

1. Place raspberries in food processor fitted with steel blade. Process using on/off pulsing action about 15 seconds or until raspberries resemble coarse crumbs.

2. Add sugar; process using on/off pulsing action until smooth. With processor running, add cream; process until well blended. Serve immediately.

Makes 3 servings

Variation: Substitute other fruits such as strawberries for the raspberries.

Sweetheart Kisses® Cookies

Sugar Cookie Dough (purchased or your favorite recipe)
HERSHEY'S Cocoa
48 HERSHEY'S KISSES® Brand Milk Chocolates, unwrapped*
1 teaspoon shortening (do not use butter, margarine, spread or oil)

*Forty-eight KISSES® Brand Milk Chocolates is enough to garnish about 3 dozen cookies following these directions; adjust as necessary for sugar cookie recipe.

1. Heat oven as directed for sugar cookies. Divide dough in half; roll out one half at a time to ¼-inch thickness following package or recipe directions. Cut out with 2-inch heart shaped cookie cutters; place on ungreased cookie sheet.

2. Bake according to package or recipe directions. Cool completely on cooling racks. Sprinkle cookies with cocoa.

3. Place 12 chocolates and shortening in small microwave-safe bowl. Microwave on HIGH (100%) 1 minute or until chocolates are melted and mixture is smooth when stirred. Drizzle over cookies. Before drizzle sets, place 1 chocolate in center of each heart.

Yield will vary according to cookie recipe used

Angel Food Cake with Pineapple Sauce

Prep Time: 10 minutes   *Cook Time: 5 minutes*

1 can (20 ounces) DOLE® Crushed Pineapple, undrained
2 tablespoons sugar
1 tablespoon cornstarch
1 tablespoon orange marmalade, peach or apricot fruit spread
1 prepared angel food cake

• Combine crushed pineapple with juice, sugar, cornstarch and orange marmalade in small saucepan. Bring to a boil. Reduce heat to low; cook, stirring constantly, 2 minutes or until sauce thickens. Cool slightly. Sauce can be served warm or chilled.

• Cut angel food cake into 12 slices. To serve, spoon sauce over each slice.

Makes 12 servings

Ultimate Chocolate Dip

Prep Time: 5 minutes   *Cook Time: 10 minutes*

⅔ cup KARO® Light Corn Syrup
½ cup heavy cream
1 (8-ounce) package semisweet chocolate or 1½ cups semisweet chocolate chips
Fresh fruit, marshmallows, brownies or cookies, as desired

In medium saucepan combine Karo and cream. Bring it to a boil over medium heat.

Remove from heat. Add chocolate and stir until melted.

Serve warm, dipping fruit, marshmallows, brownies or cookies, as desired.

MICROWAVE INSTRUCTIONS: In medium microwavable bowl stir Karo and cream. Microwave on High (100%), 1½ minutes or until boiling. Add chocolate; stir until melted.

Makes 2 cups

Delectable Desserts

Hugs® & Kisses® Crescents

1 package (8 ounces) refrigerated crescent dinner rolls
24 HERSHEY'S KISSES® Brand Milk Chocolates or HERSHEY'S
    HUGS® Chocolates
Powdered sugar

1. Heat oven to 375°F. Separate dough into 8 triangles. Remove wrappers from chocolates.

2. Place 3 chocolates at center of wide end of each triangle; chocolates on each piece of dough should be touching one another. Starting at wide end, roll to opposite point; pinch edges to seal. Place rolls, pointed side down, on ungreased cookie sheet. Curve into crescent shape.

3. Bake 10 minutes or until lightly browned. Cool slightly; sprinkle with powdered sugar. Serve warm.   *Makes 8 crescents*

NOTE: Leftover crescents can be reheated in microwave for a few seconds.

Strawberry Granita

1 quart fresh strawberries, sliced
¼ cup powdered sugar
¼ cup water
2 tablespoons sugar substitute*
1 to 1½ tablespoons fresh lemon juice, divided
½ cup fat-free whipped topping (optional)

*This recipe was tested with sucralose-based sugar substitute.

1. Combine strawberries, powdered sugar, water, sugar substitute, 1 tablespoon lemon juice in blender container. Puree. Taste; if too sweet, add additional ½ tablespoon lemon juice.

2. Pour into 8-inch metal square pan. Cover pan with foil and place in freezer. Freeze granita 2 hours or until slushy. Remove from freezer and stir to break mixture up into small chunks. Cover and return to freezer. Freeze 2 hours then stir to break granita up again. Cover and freeze at least 4 hours or overnight.

3. To serve, scrape surface of granita with large metal spoon to shave off thin pieces. Spoon into individual bowls and top each serving with 1 tablespoon whipped topping, if desired. Serve immediately.   *Makes 8 servings*

Milk Chocolate Pots de Crème

2 cups (11½-ounce package) HERSHEY'S Milk Chocolate Chips
½ cup light cream
½ teaspoon vanilla extract
Sweetened whipped cream (optional)

1. Place milk chocolate chips and light cream in medium microwave-safe bowl. Microwave on HIGH (100%) 1 minute or just until chips are melted and mixture is smooth when stirred. Stir in vanilla.

2. Pour into demitasse cups or very small dessert dishes. Cover; refrigerate until firm. Serve cold with whipped cream, if desired.

Makes 6 to 8 servings

Coconut Macaroons

4 egg whites
½ teaspoon salt
1½ cups sugar substitute*
3 cups unsweetened grated coconut**

*This recipe was tested with sucralose-based sugar substitute.
**Unsweetened coconut is available in most natural food stores.

1. Preheat oven to 325°F. Spray cookie sheet with nonstick cooking spray.

2. Place egg whites and salt in medium bowl of mixer; beat on medium about 1 minute or until soft peaks form. Add sugar substitute and continue beating until stiff peaks form.

3. Fold coconut into egg whites. Drop mixture by rounded tablespoonfuls on prepared cookie sheet. Bake 25 minutes or until light brown.

Makes 24 cookies, 2 cookies per serving

Double Chocolate Sandwich Cookies

1 package (18 ounces) refrigerated sugar cookie dough
1 bar (3½ to 4 ounces) bittersweet chocolate, chopped
2 teaspoons butter
¾ cup milk chocolate chips

1. Preheat oven to 350°F. Remove dough from wrapper, keeping in log shape.

2. Cut dough into ¼-inch-thick slices. Arrange slices 2 inches apart on ungreased cookie sheets. Cut centers out of half the cookies using ½-inch round cookie cutter.

3. Bake 10 to 12 minutes or until edges are lightly browned. Let stand on cookie sheets 2 minutes. Remove to wire rack; cool completely.

4. Place bittersweet chocolate and butter in small heavy saucepan. Heat over low heat, stirring frequently, until chocolate is melted. Spread chocolate over flat sides of cookies without holes. Immediately top each with cutout cookie.

5. Place milk chocolate chips in resealable food storage bag; seal bag. Microwave at MEDIUM (50% power) 1½ minutes. Turn bag over; microwave 1 to 1½ minutes more or until melted. Knead bag until chocolate is smooth. Cut tiny corner off bag; drizzle chocolate decoratively over sandwich cookies. Let stand until chocolate is set, about 30 minutes.

Makes 16 sandwich cookies

Berry-licious Parfait

2 cups lowfat vanilla STONYFIELD FARM® Yogurt
1 cup fresh strawberries, sliced
½ cup fresh blueberries
6 tablespoons granola

Clean and cut the strawberries into quarters, mixing them with the blueberries. Using a tall glass, alternate layers, first beginning with yogurt, then berries, and then yogurt again. Repeat this layering until the glass is full. Top with granola and enjoy.

Makes 2 parfaits

Chocolate Peanut Butter
Ice Cream Sandwiches

2 tablespoons creamy peanut butter
8 chocolate wafer cookies
⅔ cup vanilla ice cream, softened

1. Spread peanut butter over flat sides of all cookies.

2. Spoon ice cream over peanut butter on 4 cookies. Top with remaining 4 cookies, peanut butter sides down. Press down lightly to force ice cream to edges of sandwich.

3. Wrap each sandwich in foil; seal tightly. Freeze at least 2 hours or up to 5 days.

Makes 4 servings

Cream Cheese Chocolate Chip
Pastry Cookies

1 package (17.25 ounces) frozen puff pastry sheets, thawed
1 package (8 ounces) cream cheese, softened
3 tablespoons granulated sugar
1¾ cups (11.5-ounce package) NESTLÉ® TOLL HOUSE® Milk
    Chocolate Morsels, *divided*

UNFOLD *1* puff pastry sheet on lightly floured surface. Roll out to make 14×10-inch rectangle. Combine cream cheese and sugar in small bowl until smooth. Spread *half* of cream cheese mixture over pastry, leaving 1-inch border on one long side. Sprinkle with *half* of morsels. Roll up puff pastry starting at long side covered with cream cheese. Seal end by moistening with water. Repeat steps with *remaining* ingredients. Refrigerate for 1 hour.

PREHEAT oven to 375°F. Lightly grease baking sheets or line with parchment paper.

CUT rolls crosswise into 1-inch-thick slices. Place cut side down on prepared baking sheets.

BAKE for 20 to 25 minutes or until golden brown. Cool on baking sheets for 2 minutes; remove to wire racks to cool completely.

Makes about 2 dozen cookies

Acknowledgments

The publisher would like to thank the companies and organizations listed below for the use of their recipes and photographs in this publication.

ACH Food Companies, Inc.

Alouette® Cheese, Chavrie® Cheese, Saladena®

Birds Eye Foods

Crisco is a registered trademark of The J.M. Smucker Company

Cucina Classica Italiana, Inc.

Del Monte Corporation

Dole Food Company, Inc.

Eagle Brand®

Florida Department of Agriculture and Consumer Services, Bureau of Seafood and Aquaculture

The Hershey Company

The Hidden Valley® Food Products Company

Jennie-O Turkey Store®

Lawry's® Foods

McIlhenny Company (TABASCO® brand Pepper Sauce)

Nestlé USA

Reckitt Benckiser Inc.

Stonyfield Farm®

The Sugar Association, Inc.

Unilever Foods North America

USA Dry Pea & Lentil Council

Index

METRIC CONVERSION CHART

VOLUME MEASUREMENTS (dry)

⅛ teaspoon = 0.5 mL
¼ teaspoon = 1 mL
½ teaspoon = 2 mL
¾ teaspoon = 4 mL
1 teaspoon = 5 mL
1 tablespoon = 15 mL
2 tablespoons = 30 mL
¼ cup = 60 mL
⅓ cup = 75 mL
½ cup = 125 mL
⅔ cup = 150 mL
¾ cup = 175 mL
1 cup = 250 mL
2 cups = 1 pint = 500 mL
3 cups = 750 mL
4 cups = 1 quart = 1 L

VOLUME MEASUREMENTS (fluid)

1 fluid ounce (2 tablespoons) = 30 mL
4 fluid ounces (½ cup) = 125 mL
8 fluid ounces (1 cup) = 250 mL
12 fluid ounces (1½ cups) = 375 mL
16 fluid ounces (2 cups) = 500 mL

WEIGHTS (mass)

½ ounce = 15 g
1 ounce = 30 g
3 ounces = 90 g
4 ounces = 120 g
8 ounces = 225 g
10 ounces = 285 g
12 ounces = 360 g
16 ounces = 1 pound = 450 g

DIMENSIONS

1/16 inch = 2 mm
⅛ inch = 3 mm
¼ inch = 6 mm
½ inch = 1.5 cm
¾ inch = 2 cm
1 inch = 2.5 cm

OVEN TEMPERATURES

250°F = 120°C
275°F = 140°C
300°F = 150°C
325°F = 160°C
350°F = 180°C
375°F = 190°C
400°F = 200°C
425°F = 220°C
450°F = 230°C

BAKING PAN SIZES

Utensil	Size in Inches/Quarts	Metric Volume	Size in Centimeters
Baking or	8×8×2	2 L	20×20×5
Cake Pan	9×9×2	2.5 L	23×23×5
(square or	12×8×2	3 L	30×20×5
rectangular)	13×9×2	3.5 L	33×23×5
Loaf Pan	8×4×3	1.5 L	20×10×7
	9×5×3	2 L	23×13×7
Round Layer	8×1½	1.2 L	20×4
Cake Pan	9×1½	1.5 L	23×4
Pie Plate	8×1¼	750 mL	20×3
	9×1¼	1 L	23×3
Baking Dish	1 quart	1 L	—
or Casserole	1½ quart	1.5 L	—
	2 quart	2 L	—